WHEN YOUR INTRO

Understanding and Supporting the Introverted Child: A Guide for Parents and Caregivers

KAROLIN URNER

Disclaimer: The information in this book is intended for educational and informational purposes only and is not intended as medical advice. Consult with your healthcare provider before starting any new diet or exercise program.

TABLE OF CONTENTS

I. Definition of introverted child

A. The Psychology behind introverts

B. Importance of understanding and supporting introverted children

Understanding and supporting introverted children is essential for their well-being, as well as for the strength and diversity of our communities. By valuing introverted children for who they are, and providing them with the support and guidance they need to thrive, we can help them to reach their full potential and contribute their unique talents to the world.

2. Characteristics of an Introverted Child

A. Shyness

B. Sensitivity

C. Self-Awareness

D. Reflectiveness

E. Preference for Solitude

3. Challenges Faced by Introverted Children

A. Misunderstanding and Stigmatization

B. Pressure to Conform

C. Social Anxiety

D. Lack of Opportunities to Express Themselves

Introverted children may face a range of challenges in social settings. However, with understanding and support from parents, teachers, and peers, introverted children can learn to embrace their unique strengths and thrive in their own way

4. How to Support an Introverted Child

A. Respect their Boundaries

B. Create a Safe Space

C. Encourage Self-Expression

D. Foster Independence

E. Provide Opportunities for Socializing

Supporting an introverted child involves creating a safe and nurturing environment, respecting their boundaries, encouraging self-expression, fostering independence, and providing opportunities for socializing. By honoring and validating the child's natural tendencies and providing support and understanding, parents and caregivers can help introverted children thrive and reach their full potential.

5. Strategies for Helping Introverted Children Cope in Different Settings

A. School

B. Home

C. Social Events

D. Extracurricular Activities

By respecting their boundaries, creating safe spaces, encouraging self-expression, fostering independence, and providing opportunities for socializing, you can help your introverted child thrive in different settings.

6. Things to know while raising an introvert child in an extroverted environment

it is important for parents and caregivers to recognize the strengths of introverted children. Introverted children often possess qualities such as creativity, empathy, and a strong sense of self-awareness. By recognizing these strengths and providing

7. Conclusion

A. Final thoughts and recommendations for parents and caregivers.

In summary, supporting introverted children requires a multifaceted approach that prioritizes understanding, communication, validation, and encouragement. By providing a supportive and nurturing environment, parents and caregivers can help introverted children feel seen, heard, and valued, and can help them thrive both socially and emotionally

INTRODUCTION

As the sun set behind the tall trees, casting shadows across the park, a young boy sat alone on a bench, lost in thought. He was a quiet and reserved child, who often found himself lost in his own world, away from the noise and chaos of the outside world. This was not a new experience for him, as he had always been this way since he was a young child.

His parents, who were both outgoing and extroverted, found it difficult to understand their son's introverted nature. They constantly pushed him to be more outgoing and sociable, which only made him retreat further into his shell. This often led to arguments and misunderstandings, leaving the boy feeling isolated and alone.

The boy's name was Ethan, and he was a shy and sensitive child who struggled to find his place in the world. He found comfort in reading books and spending time alone in nature, where he could be himself without the pressure of having to fit in. However, as he grew older, he began to realize that his introverted nature was not accepted by those around him.

At school, Ethan often found himself struggling to make friends, as he felt uncomfortable in large groups and social situations. He preferred the company of a few close friends, who shared his interests and values. However, this often led to him being excluded from social events and gatherings, leaving him feeling left out and isolated.

As Ethan grew older, he began to understand that his introverted nature was not a weakness, but rather a strength. He realized that he had a unique perspective on the world, and that he could use his quiet strength to make a difference in the lives of others. He started to write stories and poetry, expressing his thoughts and feelings in a way that he never could in social situations.

Despite the challenges he faced, Ethan never gave up on himself. He continued to pursue his passions, and eventually found his calling in the field of psychology. He used his own experiences to help others who struggled with similar issues, and became a champion for introverted children around the world.

Ethan's story is a powerful reminder that introverted children are not broken, and do not need to be fixed. They have their own unique strengths and talents, which should be celebrated and nurtured. With the right support and guidance, introverted children can learn to embrace their inner selves, and find their place in the world.

CHAPTER ONE

- ✓ Definition of introverted child
- ✓ The Psychology behind introverts
- ✓ Importance of understanding and supporting introverted children

DEFINITION OF AN INTROVERTED CHILD

In a world that often values extroversion and gregariousness, it can be easy to overlook the unique gifts and strengths of introverted individuals. Introverts, who often prefer quiet reflection to socializing, are sometimes viewed as shy, anti-social, or even unfriendly. However, this couldn't be further from the truth.

Introverted individuals bring a wealth of talents and qualities to the table, including creativity, thoughtfulness, and a deep capacity for empathy. These qualities are especially valuable in children, who are still discovering who they are and what they want to contribute to the world.

Despite this, many introverted children struggle to thrive in environments that are designed to cater to extroverted personalities. Schools, social events, and extracurricular activities often place a premium on socializing and teamwork, leaving introverted children feeling left out and misunderstood.

As parents, caregivers, and educators, it's important that we recognize the unique needs and strengths of introverted children, and provide them with the support and guidance they need to flourish. By creating environments that value quiet contemplation, individuality, and creativity, we can help introverted children to develop a sense of self-worth, confidence, and resilience.

Definition of introverted child:

An introverted child is one who tends to be reflective, reserved, and often prefers solitude or quiet activities over socializing. They tend to be more focused on their inner world of thoughts and feelings, and may feel overwhelmed or drained by too much external stimulation. Introverted children are not necessarily shy or anti-social, but they may require more time and space to recharge and process information.

Introverted children often possess a rich inner world and a vivid imagination. They may enjoy activities such as reading, writing, drawing, or playing music, which allow them to explore their creativity and express themselves. They may also be highly observant and attuned to subtle changes in their environment or the emotions of those around them.

While introverted children may not seek out social interactions as frequently as their extroverted peers, they still crave connection and relationships. However, they may feel more comfortable with smaller, more intimate groups of friends or family members, and may prefer activities that allow for deeper conversations and meaningful connections.

Despite the many strengths and talents that introverted children possess, they may face challenges in social situations or in environments that prioritize extroverted personalities. For example, they may struggle to assert themselves in group discussions, or may feel overwhelmed by the noise and activity level of a busy classroom. They may also be more sensitive to criticism or rejection, and may need more time to process and recover from these experiences.

Understanding and supporting introverted children is essential for their well-being and success. By recognizing and celebrating their unique personalities and talents, we can help them to build their confidence and self-esteem. We can also provide them with opportunities to connect with others in ways that are comfortable and meaningful for them, and help them to develop strategies for managing challenging social situations.

In short, introverted children are a valuable and important part of our communities and should be appreciated for their unique strengths and personalities. By understanding and supporting them, we can help them to thrive and reach their full potential.

Psychology behind Introverts

The psychology behind introverts centers around the idea that introverted individuals have a unique way of processing information and interacting with the world around them. Introverts tend to be more reflective, thoughtful, and introspective than their extroverted counterparts. They prefer to take their time to process information and may need quieter and solitude to recharge their energy.

According to some theories, introversion is linked to differences in brain activity and neurotransmitter levels. Specifically, introverts may have higher levels of activity in the prefrontal cortex, which is involved in complex cognitive processes such as decision-making and problem-solving. They may also have lower levels of dopamine, a neurotransmitter associated with reward and motivation.

Another key aspect of the psychology behind introverts is the way they approach social interactions. Unlike extroverts who tend to thrive in social situations, introverts may find socializing to be draining and may need to recharge after spending time with others. They may also be more selective about the people they choose to spend time with, preferring deeper, more meaningful connections over superficial interactions.

Overall, the psychology behind introverts is complex and multifaceted. While introversion is often seen as a trait or characteristic, it is important to remember that introverted individuals are not all the same. Each person has their own unique experiences, perspectives, and preferences that shape their introverted nature. Understanding the psychology behind introverts can help us appreciate and support the unique strengths and challenges of introverted individuals.

Importance of understanding and supporting introverted children:

Understanding and supporting introverted children is crucial for several reasons. First, it's important to recognize that introversion is not a weakness or a flaw. It's simply a personality trait, and one that can bring many strengths and talents to the table. By acknowledging and celebrating introverted children for who they are, we can help to build their confidence and self-esteem.

Secondly, supporting introverted children can help to prevent them from feeling isolated or excluded from social activities. While introverted children may not enjoy large group activities or boisterous social events, they still need opportunities to connect with others and build relationships. By providing them with activities and environments that are more conducive to their personalities, we can help them to feel included and valued.

Finally, supporting introverted children can help to create a more diverse and inclusive community. By recognizing the unique needs and strengths of introverted children, we can help to create a culture that values and respects different personalities and ways of being. This can lead to more creative problem-solving, better communication, and a more positive and supportive environment for everyone.

In conclusion, understanding and supporting introverted children is essential for their well-being, as well as for the strength and diversity of our communities. By valuing introverted children for who they are, and providing them with the support and guidance they need to thrive, we can help them to reach their full potential and contribute their unique talents to the world.

CHAPTER TWO

CHARACTERISTICS OF AN INTROVERTED CHILD

- ✓ Shyness
- ✓ Sensitivity
- ✓ Self-Awareness
- ✓ Reflectiveness
- ✓ Preference for Solitude

Shyness

One of the most common characteristics of an introverted child is shyness. Shyness can manifest as a reluctance to speak up in social situations, a tendency to avoid eye contact or physical touch, and an overall sense of nervousness or apprehension around others. Shyness can be especially difficult for introverted children, as they may feel pressure to conform to social expectations and engage in extroverted behaviors.

For example, consider a quiet, reserved child who is asked to give a presentation in front of their class. This child may feel overwhelmed and anxious at the thought of standing in front of a large group, and may struggle to articulate their thoughts or ideas clearly. They may also worry about being judged or criticized by their peers, which can further exacerbate their anxiety.

Sensitivity

Introverted children are often highly sensitive to their environment and the emotions of those around them. They may pick up on subtle cues that others miss, and may be deeply affected by the moods or energy levels of people in their vicinity. This sensitivity can be both a strength and a challenge for introverted children, as it allows them to empathize with others and connect on a deeper level, but can also leave them feeling overwhelmed or drained.

Picture a sensitive introverted child who is sitting in a crowded, noisy classroom. This child may become easily distracted by the sounds and movements around them, and may feel agitated or irritable as a result. Alternatively, this child may be deeply affected by the emotional states of their classmates, and may feel sad or anxious when others are upset.

Self-Awareness

Introverted children tend to be highly introspective and self-aware. They may spend a lot of time thinking about their own thoughts, feelings, and experiences, and may be able to articulate these internal states in a clear and insightful way. This self-awareness can be a powerful tool for introverted children, as it allows them to understand themselves on a deeper level and communicate their needs effectively.

For example, An introverted child who recognizes that they need alone time to recharge their batteries. This child may be able to communicate this need to their caregivers or teachers, and may be able to negotiate a schedule or routine that allows for regular periods of solitude. This ability to advocate for oneself is a valuable skill for introverted children, as it can help them to set boundaries and manage their own energy levels effectively.

Reflectiveness

Reflectiveness is a common characteristic of introverted children. They tend to be introspective and reflective, and spend time thinking about their own thoughts and feelings. They may be more likely to analyze their experiences and understand their own emotions in greater depth. Introverted children may need time to process their thoughts and feelings, and may feel overwhelmed or anxious in highly stimulating environments.

For example, an introverted child may prefer to spend time alone after a busy day at school to recharge their energy and process their emotions. They may be more likely to journal, write, meditate, or engage in other reflective activities as a way of processing their thoughts and emotions.

Preference for Solitude

Another common trait of introverted children is a preference for solitude. Introverted children tend to feel more comfortable and relaxed in quiet, low-key environments where they can engage in solitary activities. They may be less interested in participating in group activities or spending time with large groups of people.

For example, an introverted child may enjoy spending time alone reading, drawing, or playing with toys. They may feel overwhelmed or stressed in highly stimulating environments like crowded playgrounds or noisy classrooms. Introverted children may need time alone to recharge and feel refreshed, and may benefit from having a quiet space to retreat to when they feel overstimulated or anxious.

CHAPTER THREE

CHALLENGES FACED BY INTROVERTED CHILDREN

- ✓ Misunderstanding and Stigmatization
- ✓ Pressure to Conform
- ✓ Social Anxiety
- ✓ Lack of Opportunities to Express Themselves

Misunderstanding and Stigmatization

One of the main challenges faced by introverted children is misunderstanding and stigmatization. Many people assume that introversion is a negative trait and view introverted children as shy, aloof, or unfriendly. This can lead to negative stereotypes and social stigma, which can be damaging to the child's self-esteem and social development.

Misunderstanding and stigmatization can be particularly harmful for introverted children who may already feel self-conscious or misunderstood. They may feel like they are being judged or stereotyped based on their personality type, which can lead to feelings of shame, insecurity, and a sense of being different or abnormal.

Misunderstanding and stigmatization can also have negative effects on the child's social development. Introverted children may feel like they are being excluded or overlooked by their peers, or may struggle to make meaningful social connections due to negative stereotypes and assumptions about their personality. This can lead to feelings of loneliness and isolation, which can further exacerbate negative feelings about their introverted tendencies.

To help introverted children overcome misunderstanding and stigmatization, parents and teachers can work to educate others about the positive aspects of introversion. This may involve explaining that introverted children are not necessarily shy or unfriendly, but may simply prefer to spend time alone or in quieter social settings. Parents and teachers can also encourage others to respect and honor the child's natural tendencies and preferences, rather than trying to change or "fix" them.

Additionally, parents and teachers can provide support and validation to introverted children who may be struggling with negative stereotypes or stigma. This may involve helping the child develop a strong sense of self-worth and self-confidence, and providing opportunities for the child to express themselves in ways that feel comfortable and authentic.

Ultimately, it's important to remember that introverted children have unique strengths and abilities that should be celebrated and encouraged. By challenging negative stereotypes and providing support and understanding, we can help introverted children thrive and reach their full potential.

Case study: Sarah is a quiet and reserved 8-year-old girl who enjoys spending time alone reading and drawing. Her classmates often tease her for being "weird" and "antisocial," which makes her feel embarrassed and isolated. Sarah's parents and teachers try to encourage her to be more outgoing and social, but she finds it difficult to fit in with her extroverted peers.

Pressure to Conform

Another challenge faced by introverted children is pressure to conform to social norms and expectations. In many cultures, extroversion is valued over introversion, which can lead to pressure for introverted children to be more outgoing and social. This can be stressful and overwhelming for introverted children, who may feel like they are being forced to act in ways that are uncomfortable or unnatural for them.

The pressure to conform can be particularly challenging for introverted children who have a strong sense of individuality and value their own unique way of being in the world. They may feel like they are being forced to suppress their natural tendencies and adopt behaviors that feel inauthentic to them. This can lead to feelings of frustration, anxiety, and a sense of disconnection from their true selves.

The pressure to conform can also be reinforced by social interactions and expectations at school and in other settings. Introverted children may be expected to participate in group activities, speak up in class, and engage in other behaviors that may be uncomfortable or overwhelming for them. This can lead to feelings of inadequacy or self-doubt, as well as a sense of being different or abnormal.

To help introverted children navigate the pressure to conform, parents and teachers can provide support and understanding. This may involve encouraging the child to embrace their unique strengths and abilities, and validating their feelings of discomfort in situations that may feel overwhelming. Parents and teachers can also work with the child to identify strategies for managing stress and anxiety related to the pressure to conform, such as mindfulness techniques or relaxation exercises.

Ultimately, it's important to remember that introverted children have unique personalities and ways of being in the world that should be celebrated and encouraged. While it's important to help children develop social skills and confidence, it's equally important to respect and honor their natural tendencies and preferences. By doing so, we can help introverted children thrive and reach their full potential.

Case study: James is a thoughtful and introspective 10-year-old boy who prefers to spend time alone reading and playing video games. His parents and teachers often encourage him to be more outgoing and social, which makes him feel anxious and stressed. James feels like he is being pressured to act in ways that are not true to his personality, and he struggles to fit in with his extroverted peers.

Social Anxiety:

Introverted children may also be more susceptible to social anxiety, which is a fear of social situations and interactions. This can be especially challenging for introverted children who are expected to be more outgoing and social. Social anxiety can lead to feelings of fear, embarrassment, and isolation, and can interfere with the child's ability to form meaningful social relationships.

In addition to physical symptoms, social anxiety can also cause significant emotional distress for children. Introverted children with social anxiety may feel intense fear, embarrassment, or shame in social situations. They may worry about being judged or rejected by others, and may be hyper-aware of their own perceived social inadequacies.

For introverted children with social anxiety, the fear of social situations can be a significant barrier to developing meaningful social relationships. They may avoid social situations altogether or only participate in them reluctantly, which can make it difficult to form close friendships or feel a sense of belonging within a peer group. This can lead to feelings of isolation and loneliness, which can further exacerbate social anxiety symptoms.

To help introverted children with social anxiety, parents and teachers can provide support and encouragement in social situations. This may involve gradually exposing the child to social situations in a controlled and supportive environment, such as through small group activities or one-on-one social interactions. Additionally, parents and teachers can help children develop coping strategies for managing social anxiety symptoms, such as deep breathing or positive self-talk.

It's important to recognize that social anxiety is a real and debilitating condition that requires professional support and intervention in some cases. If a child's social anxiety is severe or interfering with their daily functioning, parents and teachers may consider seeking the help of a mental health professional to develop a treatment plan.

Ultimately, it's important to remember that introverted children with social anxiety have unique strengths and abilities that should be celebrated and encouraged. With the right support and understanding, introverted children can learn to manage their social anxiety symptoms and form meaningful relationships with others.

Case study: Emily is a quiet and introspective 12-year-old girl who struggles with social anxiety. She finds it difficult to make friends and often feels anxious and self-conscious in social situations. Emily's parents and teachers try to encourage her to be more outgoing and social, but she finds it overwhelming and stressful.

Lack of Opportunities to Express Themselves:

Finally, introverted children may struggle with a lack of opportunities to express themselves. In many cases, extroverted children may dominate social interactions, which can make it difficult for introverted children to share their thoughts and feelings. This can lead to feelings of frustration and isolation, and can hinder the child's emotional development.

Introverted children often find it challenging to express themselves, as they may feel overshadowed by more outgoing peers. In many social situations, extroverted children may dominate group discussions and activities, leaving little room for introverted children to share their thoughts and feelings. This can lead to feelings of frustration and isolation, as introverted children may struggle to find their place in social settings.

For introverted children, self-expression is an important part of emotional development. Through self-expression, children can explore their thoughts and feelings, develop their creative skills, and build confidence in their own abilities. However, when introverted children are unable to express themselves, they may miss out on these valuable developmental opportunities.

One reason that introverted children may struggle to express themselves is that they may feel uncomfortable in group settings. Group discussions can be overwhelming for introverted children, who may prefer to listen and reflect rather than jump in and participate. This can lead to feelings of anxiety and self-doubt, which may further inhibit their ability to express themselves.

Another challenge faced by introverted children is that they may feel like their ideas and opinions are not valued by others. In group settings, extroverted children may dominate the conversation, leaving little room for introverted children to share their perspectives. This can be discouraging for introverted children, who may feel like their contributions are not appreciated or understood.

To help introverted children overcome these challenges, parents and teachers can provide opportunities for individual self-expression. This may involve encouraging children to engage in activities that allow them to work independently, such as writing, drawing, or other creative pursuits. Additionally, parents and teachers can help introverted children develop their communication skills by providing opportunities for one-on-one conversations and activities.

It's important to recognize that introverted children have unique strengths and abilities that should be valued and encouraged. By providing a supportive and understanding environment, parents and teachers can help introverted children develop their self-expression skills and thrive in their own way.

Case study: David is a quiet and reflective 9-year-old boy who enjoys writing and drawing. However, he often feels like his classmates don't listen to him or value his ideas. David's teachers try to encourage class participation, but he finds it difficult to speak up in a group setting. As a result, David may miss out on opportunities to express himself and develop his creative skills.

Overall, introverted children may face a range of challenges in social settings. However, with understanding and support from parents, teachers, and peers, introverted children can learn to embrace their unique strengths and thrive in their own way.

CHAPTER FOUR

HOW TO SUPPORT AN INTROVERTED CHILD

- ✓ Respect their Boundaries
- ✓ Create a Safe Space
- ✓ Encourage Self-Expression
- ✓ Foster Independence
- ✓ Provide Opportunities for Socializing

Introverted children may face a range of challenges as they navigate the social world, but there are several strategies that parents and caregivers can use to support and nurture their natural tendencies. Here are five ways to support an introverted child:

A. Respect their Boundaries:

One of the most important things that parents and caregivers can do to support an introverted child is to respect their boundaries. Introverted children may need more alone time or quiet time than extroverted children, and it's important to honor and validate their need for solitude. Parents can encourage their child to communicate their boundaries clearly and provide them with opportunities to recharge and decompress as needed.

For example, parents can create a designated quiet space in the home where the child can retreat to when they need a break from social interactions or stimulation. They can also encourage the child to take breaks during social events or activities if they start to feel overwhelmed or drained.

B. Create a Safe Space:

Another important way to support an introverted child is to create a safe and nurturing environment where they feel comfortable expressing themselves. This may involve creating a calm and soothing atmosphere in the home, with soft lighting, comfortable seating, and plenty of opportunities for quiet activities like reading or drawing.

Parents can also foster an atmosphere of acceptance and non-judgment, where the child feels free to express themselves without fear of criticism or rejection. They can encourage the child to share their thoughts and feelings in a safe and supportive environment, and provide positive feedback and validation for their ideas and perspectives.

C. Encourage Self-Expression:

Introverted children may have a rich inner world, and it's important to encourage and support their self-expression. Parents can provide opportunities for the child to explore their interests and passions, whether that means reading, writing, creating art, or pursuing other solitary activities.

They can also encourage the child to share their ideas and perspectives with others, in ways that feel comfortable and authentic. This might involve encouraging the child to write in a journal, share their thoughts with a trusted friend or family member, or express themselves through creative projects.

D. Foster Independence:

Introverted children may also benefit from opportunities to develop their independence and autonomy. Parents can encourage their child to take on new challenges and responsibilities, such as trying a new hobby or pursuing a personal goal. This can help the child build confidence in their abilities and develop a sense of self-efficacy.

Parents can also encourage the child to make their own decisions and choices, within safe and appropriate boundaries. This can help the child feel empowered and in control of their own life, which can be especially important for introverted children who may feel like they lack agency in social situations.

E. Provide Opportunities for Socializing:

While introverted children may prefer quiet and solitude, they still need opportunities for socializing and connecting with others. Parents can provide opportunities for the child to interact with others in ways that feel comfortable and authentic, such as one-on-

one conversations, small group activities, or online socializing.

It's important to respect the child's social preferences and provide opportunities that align with their natural tendencies. For example, parents can encourage the child to attend social events or activities that align with their interests or hobbies, or arrange one-on-one playdates with a close friend.

In conclusion, supporting an introverted child involves creating a safe and nurturing environment, respecting their boundaries, encouraging self-expression, fostering independence, and providing opportunities for socializing. By honoring and validating the child's natural tendencies and providing support and understanding, parents and caregivers can help introverted children thrive and reach their full potential.

CHAPTER FIVE

STRATEGIES FOR HELPING INTROVERTED CHILDREN COPE IN DIFFERENT SETTINGS

- ✓ School
- ✓ Home
- ✓ Social Events
- ✓ Extracurricular Activities

Introverted children may face various challenges in different settings, such as school, home, social events, and extracurricular activities. Here are some strategies for helping introverted children cope in each of these settings:

A. School:

1. Allow for Alone Time: Introverted children often need time alone to recharge their batteries. Encourage your child to take breaks during the school day when they need to, such as during lunchtime or recess.

2. Advocate for Your Child: Speak up for your child's needs with teachers and school administrators. Discuss how they can create a learning environment that

caters to introverted children's needs. You can also consider finding schools that are geared towards introverted children or that emphasize a low-stimulation learning environment.

3. Engage in Small Group Learning: Introverted children often excel in small group settings where they can collaborate with a few classmates. Encourage teachers to consider small group learning activities or to offer more one-on-one sessions.

4. Encourage Hobbies: Introduce your child to hobbies or activities that cater to their introverted nature, such as reading, writing, or art. It will not only help them develop their passions but also provide them with an outlet to express themselves.

B. Home:

1. Respect Your Child's Boundaries: Introverted children need space and time to themselves, so it's important to respect their boundaries when they express a need for solitude.

2. Create Quiet Spaces: Designate areas in the home where your child can go for some peace and quiet, such as a reading nook or a meditation space.

3. Encourage Relaxation Techniques: Encourage your child to develop relaxation techniques such as deep breathing, yoga, or meditation. This will not only help them relax but also teach them self-care and self-regulation skills.

4. Help them Develop Social Skills: Help your child develop their social skills by

playing games, asking open-ended questions, and encouraging them to share their thoughts and feelings.

C. Social Events:

1. Prepare in Advance: Before attending social events, discuss with your child what to expect, who they may meet, and how they can approach conversations with others.

2. Role-Play: Practice social situations with your child through role-playing to build their confidence and help them develop social skills.

3. Set Realistic Expectations: Don't force your child to attend every social event or activity. Instead, discuss with them which events are important to them and which ones they can skip.

4. Praise Efforts: Praise your child's efforts to engage in social situations, even if they don't achieve the desired outcome.

D. Extracurricular Activities:

1. Allow for Choice: Allow your child to choose extracurricular activities that cater to their interests and personality. This will encourage their participation and provide them with a sense of control.

2. Find Compatible Activities: Look for activities that cater to introverted children, such as individual sports or artistic pursuits.

3. Provide Opportunities to Socialize: While introverted children may not enjoy large group activities, they may

still enjoy socializing with like-minded individuals. Look for clubs or organizations that cater to their interests or offer opportunities for smaller group interaction.

4. Encourage Reflection: Encourage your child to reflect on their experiences and discuss what they enjoyed and what they didn't enjoy. This will help them develop self-awareness and decision-making skills.

Overall, supporting an introverted child requires patience, understanding, and a willingness to meet their needs. By respecting their boundaries, creating safe spaces, encouraging self-expression, fostering independence, and providing opportunities for socializing, you can help your introverted child thrive in different settings.

CHAPTER SIX

THINGS TO KNOW WHEN RAISING AN INTROVERT CHILD IN AN EXTROVERTED ENVIRONMENT

Raising an introverted child in an extroverted environment can be challenging for parents and caregivers. Extroverted environments, such as schools and social events, can be overwhelming for introverted children who prefer quiet and solitude. It is important to recognize the unique needs of introverted children and provide them with the support they need to thrive in their environment.

Firstly, it is important to respect an introverted child's boundaries. This means giving them the space they need to recharge their energy and not pushing them to socialize when they don't feel comfortable. Introverted children may feel overwhelmed and anxious in social situations, so it is important to allow them to take breaks and retreat to a quiet space when necessary.

Creating a safe space for introverted children is also important. This can be a space in the home where the child can go to relax and recharge their energy, or it can be a safe person the child can talk to when they need support. It is important to let introverted children know that their feelings and thoughts are valid and that they have a safe place to express them.

Encouraging self-expression is another important strategy for raising an introverted child in an extroverted environment. This can include activities such as writing, drawing, or playing an instrument. These activities provide an outlet for introverted children to express themselves without feeling overwhelmed or anxious. Encouraging self-expression can also help introverted children develop their creativity and problem-solving skills.

Fostering independence is another important strategy for raising an introverted child in an extroverted environment. Introverted children may feel more comfortable working independently, so it is important to provide them with opportunities to do so. This can include assigning tasks that the child can work on independently or providing them with books and other materials that they can explore on their own.

Providing opportunities for socializing is also important for introverted children. While introverted children may prefer solitude, it is important to help them develop their social skills and form meaningful relationships. This can include enrolling the child in activities or clubs that align with their interests or hobbies, or inviting one or two friends over for a small gathering.

It is important for parents and caregivers to communicate with their introverted child about their needs and feelings. By having open and honest conversations, parents and caregivers can better understand their child's unique needs and provide them with the support they need to thrive in an extroverted environment.

It is also important to recognize that introverted children may have different learning styles than extroverted children. While extroverted children may thrive in group settings, introverted children may prefer independent study. It is important to provide the child with learning opportunities that cater to their individual learning style.

Finally, it is important for parents and caregivers to recognize the strengths of introverted children. Introverted children often possess qualities such as creativity, empathy, and a strong sense of self-awareness. By recognizing these strengths and providing opportunities for the child to develop them, parents and caregivers can help introverted children reach their full potential.

In conclusion, raising an introverted child in an extroverted environment can be challenging, but it is possible with the right strategies and support. By respecting the child's boundaries, creating a safe space, encouraging self-expression, fostering independence, providing opportunities for socializing, communicating openly, recognizing the child's strengths, and accommodating their learning style, parents and caregivers can help introverted children thrive in their environment.

CHAPTER SEVEN

CONCLUSION

✓ Final thoughts and recommendations for parents and caregivers.

In conclusion, it is important for parents and caregivers to understand the unique needs and challenges of introverted children. By providing a supportive and understanding environment, introverted children can thrive and reach their full potential.

To further support introverted children, parents and caregivers can also encourage them to embrace their introverted nature and view it as a strength rather than a weakness. By highlighting the positive qualities associated with introversion, such as creativity, thoughtfulness, and attentiveness, parents and caregivers can help build their child's confidence and self-esteem.

It is also important for parents and caregivers to model healthy communication and boundary-setting behaviors. By setting a positive example, introverted children can learn effective communication skills and boundary-setting techniques that they can apply in various settings throughout their lives.

Moreover, parents and caregivers can provide opportunities for their child to engage in activities that align with their interests and passions. This can help foster a sense of purpose and fulfillment, which can be particularly beneficial for introverted children who may feel overwhelmed or disengaged in social situations.

Finally, parents and caregivers can educate themselves and others about the nature of introversion and the unique needs of introverted children. By challenging negative stereotypes and promoting a more nuanced understanding of introversion, parents and caregivers can help create a more inclusive and supportive environment for introverted children.

In summary, supporting introverted children requires a multifaceted approach that prioritizes understanding, communication, validation, and encouragement. By providing a supportive and nurturing environment, parents and caregivers can help introverted children feel seen, heard, and valued, and can help them thrive both socially and emotionally

Final thoughts and recommendations for parents and caregivers.

One recommendation for parents and caregivers is to prioritize communication and active listening. It is important to create an open and safe space for introverted children to express their thoughts and feelings without fear of judgment or misunderstanding. By actively listening to their concerns and validating their experiences, parents and caregivers can build trust and strengthen the relationship with their child.

Another recommendation is to provide opportunities for socializing that align with the child's interests and comfort level. This can include smaller gatherings with close friends or participation in activities that allow for solitary or independent work, such as reading or writing. By respecting the child's boundaries and preferences, parents and caregivers can help them develop a healthy balance between solitude and socializing.

Additionally, it is important to advocate for introverted children in school and extracurricular activities. This can include working with teachers and coaches to ensure that the child's needs are being met and that they are not being overlooked or misunderstood. By empowering introverted children and giving them a voice, parents and caregivers can help them feel more confident and capable in various settings.

Overall, supporting introverted children requires patience, understanding, and a willingness to adapt and accommodate to their unique needs and preferences. By prioritizing their well-being and creating a supportive environment, introverted children can thrive and reach their full potential.

Printed in Great Britain
by Amazon

27905877R00050